BASKETBALL'S GREATEST

BUZZER-BEATERS

AND OTHER CRUNCH-TIME HEROICS

BY THOM STORDEN

CAPSTONE PRESS
a capstone imprint

Captivate is published by Capstone Press, an imprint of Capstone.
1710 Roe Crest Drive, North Mankato, Minnesota 56003
www.capstonepub.com

**Library of Congress Cataloging-in-Publication Data is available on the Library
of Congress website.**
ISBN 978-1-4966-8729-6 (hardcover)
ISBN 978-1-4966-8734-0 (paperback)
ISBN 978-1-4966-8735-7 (ebook PDF)

Summary: When the clock is ticking down and the stakes are high, some players
seize the moment and make themselves legends. From buzzer-beating half-court
shots to thunderous last-second dunks, some of basketball's greatest moments are
chronicled in vivid fashion here. You've got a courtside seat to the action.

Photo Credits
AP Photo: Brett Coomer, 13, Carol Francavilla, 27, Eric Risberg, 43, Lennox
Mclendon, 33, Sue Ogrocki, 24; Getty Images: Andy Lyons, 37, Rich Clarkson, 45;
Newscom: TNS/Jane Tyska, 44, TNS/Richard W. Rodriguez, 31, TNS/Yong Kim,
41, UPI/Aaron Josefczyk, 38, USA Today Sports/Craig Mitchelldyer, 29, USA Today
Sports/John E. Sokolowski, 7, 9; Shutterstock: cristovao, cover (player), Oleksii
Sidorov, cover (arena), 1; silvae, cover (lights), 1; Sports Illustrated: Bob Rosato, 35,
Damian Strohmeyer, 15, 21, 22, John Biever, 5, John W. McDonough, 11, Manny
Millan, 17, 19

Editorial Credits
Bobbie Nuytten, designer; Eric Gohl, media researcher; Katy LaVigne, production
specialist

TABLE OF CONTENTS

Words in **bold** are in the glossary.

A CLOCK, A BALL, AND A NET

One of the most exciting elements of the game of basketball is the ever-ticking clock. Time is always moving. The end is always near. And when that clock winds down, the stars come out. Maybe it's Magic Johnson or Steph Curry heaving in a **buzzer-beater** from beyond half-court. Maybe it's Arike Ogunbowale hitting a winning shot at the final horn. Maybe it's Damian Lillard nailing a crunch-time three. Or LeBron James fly-swatting a last-second layup.

Clutch plays are plays made when the game—or the season—is on the line. Any serious basketball player or fan recognizes it. For heart-thumping, spine-tingling fun, there's nothing like a big play that wins a game in crunch time.

Michael Jordan became one of basketball's all-time best players. During his career, he broke the hearts of opponents by making last-second shots more than a few times.

CHAPTER 1

EPIC BUZZER-BEATERS

BOUNCE, BOUNCE, BOUNCE

It was Game 7 of the Eastern Conference Semifinals. The winner would advance one step closer to the 2019 National Basketball Association (NBA) Finals. The loser's season would be over. The Toronto Raptors and the Philadelphia 76ers were tied at 90. Only four seconds were left to play.

The Raptors, Canada's only NBA team, had never been to the Finals. But they had one last shot, and the ball was in their best player's hands. Kawhi Leonard dribbled. He dashed to his right. Philly's two best players, Ben Simmons and Joel Embiid, were glued to Leonard.

The Toronto crowd watched as Leonard, almost out of room, reached the corner. He rose up to shoot. When he let the ball go, it seemed like an entire nation held its breath. The buzzer sounded. The backboard lights went red.

The ball floated higher than usual for a Leonard shot. But the Raptors' star forward shot it that way on purpose. Leonard knew that if he shot high, he might get a bounce.

Kawhi Leonard jumps to release his shot over Joel Imbiid of the 76ers.

Bounce it did. When the ball hit the front of the rim, it bounded straight up.

No one in Canada breathed.

When it bounced a second time, it jumped to the other side of the hoop.

No one in Canada moved.

When it bounced a third time, it looked like it might fall off the rim.

No one in Canada wanted that to happen.

When it bounced a fourth time, the ball seemed worn out, as if it had decided enough was enough. The ball dropped through the net.

No one in Canada would ever forget it.

The Raptors went on to the Finals. There, Leonard and the Raptors took down the mighty Golden State Warriors. Canada had its first NBA title.

Kawhi Leonard played only one season in Toronto. In 2019, he signed a contract with the Clippers. The Clippers are based in Leonard's hometown of Los Angeles.

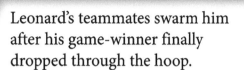

Leonard's teammates swarm him after his game-winner finally dropped through the hoop.

A REPEAT CHAMPION

Kawhi Leonard was drafted by San Antonio. He and the Spurs won the NBA Finals in 2013–14. At age 22, Leonard was named the Finals Most Valuable Player (MVP). Leonard was known for his defense. He won NBA Defensive Player of the Year twice as a Spur.

SWOON FOR SPOON

The Women's National Basketball Association (WNBA) began play in the summer of 1997. Teresa Weatherspoon was the New York Liberty's first starting point guard. It's fitting that the WNBA's most famous shot was sunk by one of its pioneers.

It was Game 2 of the best of three series of the 1999 WNBA Finals. Weatherspoon and the Liberty were down one game and two points to the Houston Comets. Only 2.4 seconds remained. The Comets' Tina Thompson had just scored the go-ahead basket. The Comets led, 67–65. The Houston crowd was going wild.

The Liberty had no time-outs. They had to think fast. Liberty center Kym Hampton held the ball under the basket. Hampton said, "I have to admit I was already sulking even before I took the ball out." But Hampton pulled it together. She passed to Weatherspoon.

Teresa Weatherspoon goes to the hoop in the WNBA Finals against the Houston Comets.

Weatherspoon knew there was one last chance. And she would be the one to take it. "I didn't want any of my teammates to have to live with missing that shot during the offseason," said Weatherspoon. "If it didn't go in, I wanted to be the one to have to live with that."

Weatherspoon turned. She headed up the court. Thompson was playing strong defense beside her. With two quick dribbles, Weatherspoon was nearing half-court. But 2.4 seconds goes fast. Weatherspoon had to launch it. From behind the half-court line, she heaved the ball. The ball arced high. The orange and white WNBA ball spun like a pinwheel.

The ball came down. It banked off the glass and went into the net. Confetti slowly tumbled to the floor as the Liberty mobbed the player lovingly nicknamed "Spoon." The Houston crowd was silenced. The Comet players stood in shock.

The Comets and the Liberty met in three of the first four WNBA Finals. The Comets franchise disbanded in 2008. The Liberty plays on.

Teammates mob Weatherspoon after her half-court shot won the game for the Liberty.

AT GREAT HEIGHTS

The Comets won the 1999 WNBA title in Game 3. The Comets were the WNBA's first **dynasty**. They won titles in the league's first four seasons. Each time, Comet guard Cynthia Cooper won Finals MVP. Cooper, Tina Thompson, and Sheryl Swoopes were the Comets' three main stars. All three women are in the Hall of Fame.

FULL-COURT FLINGS

Half-court buzzer-beaters are amazing. Three-quarter or nearly full-court shots? Astounding! Some of the NBA's greats have dialed long distance. Some more than once. Here is a starry short list of long shots.

In 1987, Lakers point guard Magic Johnson tossed in a nearly full-court shot. Launched with one hand, the shot beat the halftime buzzer. James Worthy, Magic's teammate, was impressed. "Everything is possible when he has the ball," Worthy said.

In 2001, Baron Davis of the Hornets made an 89-foot buzzer-beater. The shot came at the end of the third quarter. It is the longest shot made in an NBA game.

LeBron James hit the longest shot of his career in 2007. Playing for Cleveland, James heaved in a two-handed 80-footer against Boston. The shot beat the third-quarter horn. Without it, the Cavaliers wouldn't have won, 107–104.

Chris Bosh hit two separate buzzer-beating three-quarter court shots in 2007. The Raptors forward nailed the first shot on January 31 versus the Wizards. He did it again on November 2 against the Nets.

In 2015–16, Grizzlies guard Vince Carter drained two separate three-quarter court shots. The first came on November 27, 2015, versus the Hawks. The second came 84 days later against the Timberwolves.

In a 2015 game, Celtics forward Jae Crowder made a true full-court shot. The ball traveled 94 feet and went through the hoop. But Crowder was standing out of bounds. He was attempting to pass the ball in. The basket did not count.

LeBron James of the Cleveland Cavaliers

CHAPTER 2

ALL-TIME CLUTCH PERFORMANCES

RARE AIR

Many consider basketball's greatest player to be Michael Jordan. "Air" Jordan may be best known for his slam dunks. But without a few clutch shots, he wouldn't be considered the best ever. Two clutch shots stand out.

The first happened in 1989. Jordan and the Chicago Bulls faced the Cleveland Cavaliers. It was the fifth and final game of the opening round of the playoffs. Jordan had scored 31, 30, 44, and 50 points in the first four games.

Near the end of Game 5, Jordan already had 42 points. Three seconds remained. The Bulls were **inbounding** from half-court. The Cavs led 100–99. Everyone in Cleveland's arena knew the ball would go to Jordan. The Cavs had two defenders, Larry Nance and Craig Ehlo, covering Jordan.

Somehow, Jordan **juked** the defense. He got open. He received the pass. He dribbled to his left.

Jordan went up for a jump shot near the free-throw line. Ehlo sprang at him. But Jordan—an incredible leaper—outlasted Ehlo in midair. He seemed to almost **double-clutch** as he hung there. Jordan released. The shot rattled home. The Bulls won, 101–100, and **clinched** the series.

Michael Jordan led the Chicago Bulls into a 1989 playoff series against the talented Cleveland Cavaliers.

In 1998, Jordan's Bulls led in the NBA Finals, three games to two. They faced the Utah Jazz. Late in Game 6 in Utah, the Jazz led, 86–83. Jordan hit a driving layup to cut the lead to one. Then, on defense, he stole the ball away from Jazz star Karl Malone. Taking his sweet time, Jordan crossed half-court. The seconds melted away. With 10 seconds left, Jordan put on a burst. He blew past the Jazz defender.

Jordan launched an 18-foot shot. It swished through the net with five seconds left. Jordan left his follow-through in the air for just an extra second. It gave fans a lasting image. The Jazz couldn't score, and Jordan and the Bulls had won it all.

CAV CRUNCHER

Jordan's basket to beat Cleveland in 1989 came to be known as "The Shot." In 1993, Jordan added another beauty against the Cavs. Again, it was a playoff game. Again, it took place in Cleveland. In Game 4, with the Bulls up by three games, Jordan hit a **fadeaway** buzzer-beater. The shot came from nearly the same spot as the one he made four years earlier.

Jordan led the Bulls to six NBA titles during his career.

LINSANITY

The New York Knicks were struggling. The team's record was 8–15. New York hoops fans were not happy. On February 4, 2012, Knicks point guard Jeremy Lin got up from the bench. In his first 23 games with the Knicks, Lin played a total of only 55 minutes. But he took off his warmups. He entered the ball game. The clock showed 3:35 remaining in the first quarter. The Knicks trailed, 21–16. But things were about to change.

What happened next was a surprise. Lin started driving for layups. He threw sweet lob passes to center Tyson Chandler. The Knicks' home crowd woke up. With each basket, slick pass, or defensive steal, Lin grew bolder. His confidence rose. The Knicks surged ahead. By the game's end, Lin led all scorers with 25 points. The Knicks had won, 99–92. The Madison Square Garden crowd chanted his name.

But Lin was just warming up. Coach Mike D'Antoni put Lin into the starting lineup the next game. Again, Lin led all scorers with 28 points. He also dished out eight assists. Again, the Knicks won, beating the Jazz. The next game, Lin scored 23 with 10 assists and beat the Wizards. The game after that, Lin outdueled Kobe Bryant. Lin had 38 points to Bryant's 34. The Knicks beat the L.A. Lakers, 92–85.

Jeremy Lin drives to score in the face of the Celtics star Kevin Garnett.

In less than a week's time, Lin had seemed to come out of nowhere. He had become a hoops hero in the nation's largest city. Three more wins pushed the Knicks back to an even 15–15 record. "Linsanity" was in full effect.

Jeremy Lin emerged as a surprise star when the Knicks desperately needed one.

NBA fans and the media soon got to know Lin. He was intelligent—a Harvard University graduate. He was one of the few Asian American players in the NBA. He was a good player. He was a good guy.

Lin's season was cut short due to a knee injury. But he had turned the Knicks around. The Knicks finished the season with a winning record. They even made the playoffs. New York City would never forget.

Jeremy Lin starred at Harvard University from 2006–2010. He was a three-time All-Ivy League player. He graduated with a 3.1 grade point average and a degree in economics.

THE CURRY FLURRY

Golden State Warriors guard Stephen Curry has a baby-faced smile. He is not super tall or muscular. He doesn't have amazing speed or jumping ability. But Curry can dribble like a magician. And his shooting? Out of this world.

Curry is only halfway through his pro career. But his clutch play has already given fans hours of highlights. It has also helped the Warriors win three titles. One of the most amazing clutch games of Curry's career came in 2016. It was a contest in Oklahoma City. Going against the Thunder, Curry nailed four 3-pointers in the first half.

Steph Curry connected on 402 3-pointers in 2015–16. The number set a single-season NBA record.

In the second half, Curry sprained his ankle. But he played through the pain and made another eight treys. Curry's final three of the night was the game-winner. He shot it from 35 feet away with 0.6 seconds left in overtime. For the game, Curry tallied 46 total points. He made an amazing 12 3-pointers. That tied the record for 3-pointers in an NBA game up until that time.

"He's got the greatest range I've ever seen," said Curry's teammate, Klay Thompson, after the game. "He makes it look so effortless."

Thompson, a great shooter himself, would know. After Curry upped the record to 13, Thompson broke the single-game record for threes in 2018. Thompson hit an amazing 14 threes.

CURRYS ALL AROUND

Steph Curry's brother, Seth, and brother-in-law, Damion Lee, have both spent time in the NBA. Curry's father, Dell, also played. Dell was a slick long-range bomber in the NBA from 1986–2002. He won the NBA's Sixth Man award in 1993–94. Dell Curry retired as the Hornets' all-time leader in threes made. Overall, he made 1,245 career 3-pointers.

CHAPTER 3

BUZZER-BEATER REPEATERS

DOUBLE DEVIL

Christian Laettner is considered one of college basketball's great players. He is also considered one of the most disliked. The reason for both is the same. He was a very confident player. He believed he would win and often did.

But Laettner may be remembered best for two clutch shots. The first was in 1990. Duke faced Connecticut. A trip to the Final Four was on the line. Duke trailed 78–77 with just 2.6 seconds remaining. Laettner, a sophomore, passed the ball in on the sideline. Quickly, Laettner got the ball back. Then he hit a leaning jump shot to win the game.

In 1992, Duke played Kentucky. The winner would go to the Final Four. With 2.1 seconds left, Duke trailed 103–102. The Blue Devils had to inbound from under the *opposite* basket. Forward Grant Hill threw a long pass that any quarterback would admire.

Near the free-throw line, Laettner leaped. He snagged the pass. Giving a shoulder fake, he dribbled and whirled. Laettner launched a fadeaway jumper from 18 feet out. If his shot missed the mark, it would have been his final college shot. Laettner was a senior. The shot was true. Duke won and went on to win the **championship**.

Christian Laettner's game-winner against Kentucky became one of the most famous shots in the history of college basketball.

DEEP DAGGERS

Damian Lillard was a long shot. Coming out of high school in California, Lillard was not wanted by major college basketball programs. He got a scholarship from little-known Weber State. After four years of college, the point guard showed great progress. In 2012, the Portland Trail Blazers drafted him.

The Blazers were soon rewarded. Lillard won 2012–13 NBA Rookie of the Year. And then he started winning games with his 3-point shot. In 2014, he hit an amazing 3-pointer as time expired to clinch a playoff series victory against Houston.

In 2019, Lillard did it again. This time in a playoff series versus Oklahoma City. The score was tied, 115–115. Lillard dribbled the ball. The clock wound down. *Five, four, three . . .*

Lillard stood 10 feet beyond the 3-point line. The defender was an arm's length away. Lillard faked and stepped *back* to shoot. The crowd gasped as the long shot seemed to float. Lillard had shot from nearer half-court than the 3-point line!

Of course, Lillard's dagger found the net. The shot was a game- and series-winner. It also gave Lillard an even 50 points. Lillard's teammates stormed the court. The crowd roared. Lillard waved goodbye to Oklahoma City.

Damian Lillard shoots as time runs out against the Houston Rockets.

Damian Lillard prefers the letter "O" over "zero" when describing his jersey number. He has said that the *O* on his chest stands for lots of things. Oakland: the city of his birth. Ogden: the city in Utah where he went to college. Oregon: the state that holds Portland, the city where he plays as a pro.

CHAPTER 4

THE UNDERDOGS

BULLDOG UNDERDOGS

It was the women's college basketball tournament of 2017. Mississippi State faced Connecticut. The Bulldogs of Mississippi State were more than just **underdogs**. The Huskies from UConn were riding a 111-game winning streak. That's a streak that spanned nearly three seasons. A streak that included a 60-point victory over Mississippi State the previous season. A streak that was the longest in women's college basketball history.

But in overtime, the score was tied at 64. Time was running out. The Bulldogs had the ball. They could take the final shot. Bulldog guard Morgan William wasn't thinking about streaks. She was thinking about scoring.

The University of South Carolina played Mississippi State for the 2017 women's college championship. South Carolina won, 67–55.

William dribbled hard to the basket. She suddenly pulled up near the free-throw line. With one second left, she lofted a high floater. As the buzzer sounded, the shot hit nothing but net. Morgan and her teammates celebrated. They jumped. They hugged. They screamed. It was like they had won it all.

Morgan William led the underdog Mississippi State to an unlikely victory over the Huskies of UConn.

SAMPSON'S REVENGE

Not many folks gave the Houston Rockets a chance to upset the Lakers in the matchup to go to the 1986 Finals. The Lakers had been to the Finals for four straight seasons. But tree-topping center Ralph Sampson and the Rockets didn't care much about that.

The Lakers took Game 1 in the best-of-seven series. They won with ease, 119–107. But then the Rockets began to soar. Houston was led by its two centers: Sampson, who stood 7-foot-4, and Hakeem Olajuwon, who was a 7-footer himself. People called them "the twin towers." Amazingly, the Rockets won the next three in a row. Now Houston was up, three games to one.

The Lakers were angry. And they were still favored. They wanted to put the Rockets in their place. Late in Game 5, the teams battled. The score was knotted at 112. One second remained. The Rockets were inbounding the ball at half-court. They had a chance to knock out the big-shot Lakers.

The Rockets lobbed a pass. Sampson caught it. From an impossible angle, he shot it. The ball hit the rim. It bounced around. Finally, it dropped, as did the jaws of Lakers fans. Sampson and the Rockets ended up losing to the Celtics in the Finals. But Sampson's twisting, buzzer-beating shot was one for the ages.

Rushing to beat the clock, Ralph Sampson had to fling the ball toward the hoop.

Ralph Sampson was born and raised in Virginia. He played four star-studded years for his home-state University of Virginia Cavaliers. In 1983, the Houston Rockets made Sampson the number one overall pick in the NBA Draft.

GINÓBILI'S GEMS

Basketball was introduced as an Olympic sport at the 1936 Games held in Berlin, Germany. Games were played outdoors rather than indoors. On a clay court. With an odd, oversized ball. It wasn't what players were used to.

The final game was played through rain. This turned the clay court to mud. Still, the United States came away victorious. They bested Canada, 19–8, for the gold. Medals were handed out by the inventor of basketball, James Naismith.

The U.S. dominated Olympic basketball through the years. But in 2004 in Athens, Greece, the U.S. met its match in Argentina. This opponent featured strong passing, defense, and team play.

In the semifinal, Argentina upset the U.S., 89–81. Guard Manu Ginóbili led his country. He scored 29 points, including four timely 3-pointers. After the game, Argentina's coach spoke out. "America is the cradle of basketball," said Rubén Pablo Magnano. "Today, maybe we were lucky."

Hardly. Argentina kept up its great play. In the next game, they pounded Italy. Again, Ginóbili led the way. He led his team with six assists to go along with 16 points. With an 84–69 victory, Argentina took the gold medal.

Manu Ginóbili enjoyed a long NBA career in the U.S. The Argentinian teamed with French-born guard Tony Parker and Bahamas-born center Tim Duncan. He played 16 seasons in all. He helped the Spurs win four NBA titles.

Ginóbili puts in a layup while facing the U.S. in the semifinals of the 2004 Olympics.

CHAPTER 5

CHAMPIONSHIP HEROES

BACK-TO-BACK MIRACLES

It's one thing to hit a game-winning buzzer-beater. It's another to do it two games in a row. It's an entirely different thing to do it in the semifinal and final games. Of the biggest tournament. Of your life.

Arike Ogunbowale pulled off these feats in the span of 48 hours. The games were in the 2018 National Collegiate Athletic Association (NCAA) women's tournament. In the semifinal, the Notre Dame Fighting Irish faced the mighty Connecticut Huskies. Notre Dame was good. But the Huskies were undefeated at 36–0. The score deadlocked at 89.

The clock ticked. Just seconds remained. Ogunbowale dribbled and faked. She made her way down the sideline. After a crossover dribble and step-back jumper, she put up a shot. It ripped the net with just one second remaining. The Huskies couldn't respond. The Irish won. They were headed to the final.

Arike Ogunbowale reacts after hitting the first of her two game-winners in the 2018 NCAA tournament.

In the championship, Notre Dame found itself tied again. With three seconds remaining, the Irish were tied at 58 with Mississippi State. Ogunbowale got the ball and again dribbled right. She launched, this time behind the 3-point line.

The national championship hung in the air along with the ball. It was almost impossible to think that Ogunbowale's shot would go in. But go in it did. She was a hero.

Ogunbowale raises the trophy after leading her team to the NCAA Championship.

Afterward, Ogunbowale said, "To do that twice in one weekend, the biggest stage in basketball, it's crazy."

The next season, Ogunbowale was reminded that not every final shot is a game-winner. One year later, Ogunbowale and the Irish found themselves back in the championship game. With two seconds left, Ogunbowale was at the foul line. Notre Dame was down two. On the first shot, Ogunbowale . . . missed. Then, trying to miss so that her team could get the rebound and possibly toss in a winner, she accidentally made it. Notre Dame lost.

Arike Ogunbowale went to the Dallas Wings with the fifth pick in the 2019 WNBA Draft. The draft was held three days after Ogunbowale and Notre Dame had lost the championship. Ogunbowale led Dallas in scoring with 19.1 points per game in her rookie season.

SUPER 'NOVA

In 1985, the Villanova Wildcats took down the Georgetown Hoyas. This gave them the men's college basketball championship. The Wildcats were the underdogs. But they reached their goal with great teamwork and courage.

Thirty-one years later, another Villanova team rose to the top. These new 'Cats looked much the same as the old 'Cats. They worked together and were fearless and clutch. The Wildcats faced the North Carolina Tar Heels for the 2016 championship. With just over a minute left in the game, Villanova led by six. They appeared to have the game won. But Tar Heels guard Marcus Paige came up big. He hit not one but two big 3-pointers. The game was tied at 74.

There were just 4.7 seconds left to go. Villanova inbounded from the opposite end of the court. Wildcat guard Ryan Arcidiacono dribbled six times. He dished the ball to teammate Kris Jenkins. Without hesitating,

Jenkins rose up and unleashed a deep 3-pointer. After the ball left Jenkins' hand, the clock ran down to zero. The horn sounded. The ball was still in the air. What would happen?

Swish!

The buzzer-beating ball went through the net. The Wildcats had won their second national championship.

Two years after Kris Jenkins' buzzer-beater, the 2017–18 Villanova Wildcats won it all again. Point guard Jalen Brunson led the Wildcats. He became the only player in school history to be in the starting lineup for two championship games.

Kris Jenkins shoots as time runs short in the 2016 title game against North Carolina.

THE BLOCK

Folks in Cleveland will long remember "The Block." It came in Game 7 of the 2016 NBA Finals, when the Cleveland Cavaliers were playing the Golden State Warriors. The Cavs had been down three games to one against the Warriors, who had just finished off the best season (73–9) in NBA history. Things did not look good for Cleveland. Furthermore, no team from Cleveland had won a sports championship in 52 years.

But the Cavs and their star, LeBron James, didn't give up. The Cavs came away with gritty wins in Game 5 and Game 6. James scored 41 points in each contest. The Cavs and James were hungry. The city of Cleveland was starved.

Game 7 came down to the wire. With 100 seconds remaining, the score was tied at 89. The Warriors were out on a fast break. Warriors forward Andre Iguodala led the pack. He found a clear path to the hoop. But jetting in from out of nowhere, James came to the rescue. Nearly hitting his head on the rim, a flying James swatted Iguodala's layup attempt off the backboard. No one had ever seen such a timely block.

Moments later, the Cavs' Kyrie Irving hit a big 3-pointer. James, who notched a **triple double**, iced the game with a free throw with 10 seconds left. Thanks largely to The Block, Cleveland *finally* came through.

Always a star on offense, LeBron James made a great play on defense that will be remembered as "The Block."

▶ As of 2019, Stephen Curry currently holds the pro record for shots made from beyond half-court. He has made five such shots in NBA games. Curry, a guard, shares the record with Zach Randolph, who was a power forward. He played in the NBA from 2001 to 2018. During that time, Randolph played for five different teams.

Stephen Curry

▶ Teresa Weatherspoon has led an interesting basketball life. She was born in 1965 in Pineland, Texas. She attended Louisiana Tech University. As a senior, she led her team to the national championship. She played professionally overseas for a time. In 1997, the 31-year-old joined the WNBA. She played for the New York Liberty for eight years. Then she became a coach. Weatherspoon was named to the James Naismith Memorial Basketball Hall of Fame in 2019.

► Going into the 1972 Olympics, the U.S. men's basketball team had won 62 straight games. In fact, the U.S. had never lost in eight different Olympic Games. But in 1972, the Soviet Union beat the U.S., 51–50. The winning shot, by Alexander Belov, beat the buzzer. The U.S. protested. They said that the referees and timekeeper made mistakes. They said that the Soviets were given unfair extra chances at the last shot. But the score stood. The Soviet Union won. They were the first team not from the U.S. to win gold in basketball.

Alexander Belov takes his gold medal-winning shot.

► Wataru "Wat" Misaka broke pro basketball's color barrier. In 1947–48 Misaka became the first nonwhite professional basketball player. A 5-foot-7 guard of Japanese descent, Misaka played for the New York Knickerbockers. Before playing pro, Misaka played in college for the University of Utah. He was drafted into the U.S. Army in 1944. He spent military time in East Asia and Japan. Misaka passed away in 2019.

GLOSSARY

buzzer-beater (BUZ-er BEET-er)—a basketball shot released by the player right before game time runs out and the buzzer sounds

championship (CHAM-pee-uhn-ship)—a contest held to decide who is the champion

clinch (KLINCH)—to make certain of winning

clutch (KLUHCH)—a tight or critical situation

double-clutch (DUH-buhl-KLUHCH)—a move that involves the player changing the position of the ball in midair before shooting

dynasty (DYE-nuh-stee)—a team that wins multiple championships over a period of several years

fadeaway (FAYD-eh-way)—a basketball shot taken while the player jumps back away from the hoop

inbound (IN-baund)—to put a basketball in play by passing it onto the court from out of bounds

juke (JOOK)—to fake out an opposing player

triple double (TRIP-uhl DU-buhl)—an achievement made when a player reaches double digits in points, assists, and rebounds

underdog (UHN-der-dawg)—a person or team that is not expected to win an event

READ MORE

Frederick, Shane. *Basketball's Record Breakers*. North Mankato, MN: Capstone Press, 2017.

Omoth, Tyler. *A Superfan's Guide to Pro Basketball Teams*. North Mankato, MN: Capstone Press, 2018.

Sports Illustrated for Kids Editors. *Big Book of WHO: Basketball*. New York: Sports Illustrated for Kids, 2015.

INTERNET SITES

NBA
www.nba.com

Naismith Memorial Hall of Fame
www.hoophall.com

SOURCE NOTES

Page 10, "I have to admit …," Brian Martin, "The Shot: Teresa Weatherspoon's Magical Moment—Part I," wnba.com, Sept. 4, 2016, https://www.wnba.com/news/teresa-weatherspoon-shot-wnba-finals-oral-history-1/, Accessed March 18, 2020.

Page 12, "I didn't want any …," Ibid.

Page 14, "Everything is possible …," Gordon Edes, "Magic Throws in Miracle 80-Footer as Lakers Romp," *Los Angeles Times*, April 24, 1987, https://www.latimes.com/archives/la-xpm-1987-04-24-sp-486-story.html, Accessed March 18, 2020.

Page 25, "He's got the greatest range …," Cliff Brunt, Associated Press, "Curry Hits Winning 3, Sets Record as Warriors Beat Thunder," Feb. 28, 2016, https://apnews.com/5469f51686894803aef40376 4949405f, Accessed March 18, 2020.

Page 34, "America is the cradle of basketball," Bill Dwyre, "The Cradle of Basketball Gets Rocked at Olympics," *Los Angeles Times*, Aug. 28, 2004, https://www.latimes.com/archives/la-xpm-2004-aug-28-sp-olymenhoops28-story.html, Accessed March 18, 2020.

Page 39, "To do that twice in one weekend...," Graham Hays, "Irish's Arike Ogunbowale Hits Shot of a Lifetime ... Again," ESPN, April 1, 2018, https://www.espn.com/womens-college-basketball/story?id=22992885&_slug_=women-final-four-arike-ogunbowale-hits-shot-life-lead-notre-dame-fighting-irish-ncaa-title, Accessed March 18, 2020.

INDEX